10-12-12

M

# BATMAN
## THE DARK KNIGHT

VOLUME 1    KNIGHT TERRORS

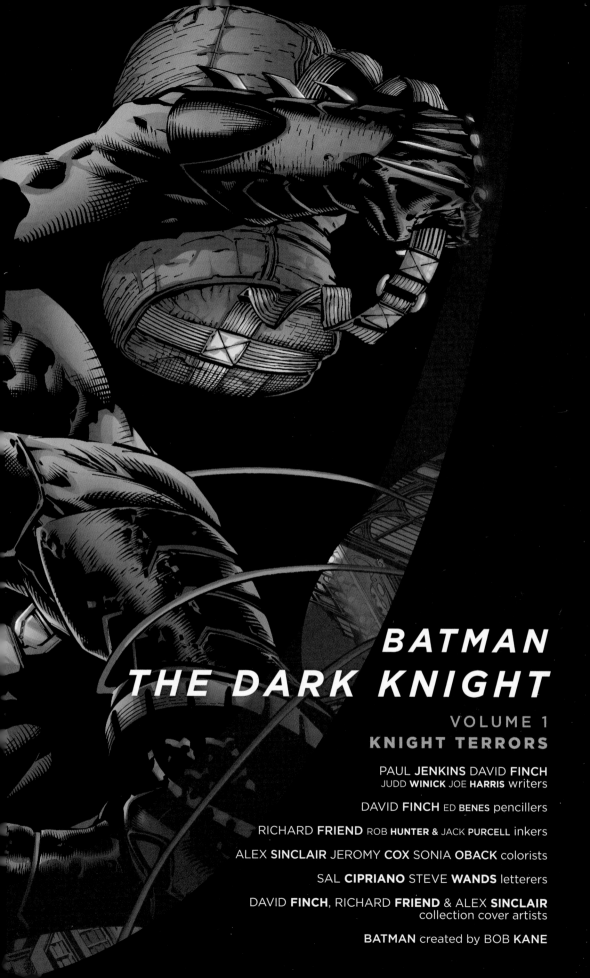

# BATMAN
# THE DARK KNIGHT

## VOLUME 1
## KNIGHT TERRORS

PAUL **JENKINS** DAVID **FINCH**
JUDD **WINICK** JOE **HARRIS** writers

DAVID **FINCH** ED **BENES** pencillers

RICHARD **FRIEND** ROB **HUNTER** & JACK **PURCELL** inkers

ALEX **SINCLAIR** JEROMY **COX** SONIA **OBACK** colorists

SAL **CIPRIANO** STEVE **WANDS** letterers

DAVID **FINCH**, RICHARD **FRIEND** & ALEX **SINCLAIR**
collection cover artists

BATMAN created by BOB **KANE**

MIKE MARTS Editor – Original Series  RICKEY PURDIN Assistant Editor – Original Series  ROWENA YOW Editor
ROBBIN BROSTERMAN Design Director – Books  ROBBIE BIEDERMAN Publication Design

BOB HARRAS VP – Editor-in-Chief

DIANE NELSON President  DAN DIDIO and JIM LEE Co-Publishers
GEOFF JOHNS Chief Creative Officer
JOHN ROOD Executive VP – Sales, Marketing and Business Development
AMY GENKINS Senior VP – Business and Legal Affairs  NAIRI GARDINER Senior VP – Finance
JEFF BOISON VP – Publishing Operations  MARK CHIARELLO VP – Art Direction and Design
JOHN CUNNINGHAM VP – Marketing  TERRI CUNNINGHAM VP – Talent Relations and Services
ALISON GILL Senior VP – Manufacturing and Operations  HANK KANALZ Senior VP – Digital
JAY KOGAN VP – Business and Legal Affairs, Publishing  JACK MAHAN VP – Business Affairs, Talent
NICK NAPOLITANO VP – Manufacturing Administration  SUE POHJA VP – Book Sales
COURTNEY SIMMONS Senior VP – Publicity  BOB WAYNE Senior VP – Sales

BATMAN THE DARK KNIGHT VOLUME 1: KNIGHT TERRORS

DC Comics, 1700 Broadway, New York, NY 10019
A Warner Bros. Entertainment Company
Printed by RR Donnelley, Salem, VA, USA. 8/31/12. First Printing.

HC ISBN: 978-1-4012-3543-7
SC ISBN: 978-1-4012-3711-0

Library of Congress Cataloging-in-Publication Data

Finch, David, 1972-
Batman, the dark knight. Volume 1, Knight terrors / David Finch, Paul Jenkins, Richard Friend.
p. cm.
"Originally published in single magazine form in Batman: The Dark Knight 1-9."
ISBN 978-1-4012-3543-7
1. Graphic novels. I. Jenkins, Paul, 1965- II. Friend, Richard (Illustrator) III. Title. IV. Title: Knight terrors.
PN6728.B36F46 2012
741.5'973—dc23
2012022442

# KNIGHT TERRORS

PAUL JENKINS writer/co-plotter   DAVID FINCH penciller/co-plotter   RICHARD FRIEND inker

cover art by DAVID FINCH, RICHARD FRIEND & ALEX SINCLAIR

GOTHAM CITY.

Fear is a cannibal that feeds upon itself.

It lives in every dark shadow-- waits around every corner.

It can be in two places at once...on the path ahead, yet somehow always *behind* you.

Fear hides in every decision, questioning your every move. And it's your fault.

You are the one who gives it life.

DEET

You are the parent of your own fear.

Every instinct tells us we can do nothing in the face of that which terrifies us.

But that's what fear is--*instinct*.

We run because that is our nature. Better to run away and live to fight another day, or so the saying goes.

But if we run, the cannibal feeds and grows stronger.

*PAF*

Better to run towards your fear. Better still to *face* it.

Stare it in the eye. Make it blink.

Watch it shrink.

A FINE SPEECH, *MR. WAYNE.* WISH I COULD SHARE YOUR SENTIMENTS, BUT GIVEN THE ECONOMY AND THE LATEST JOBLESS FIGURES COMING OFF THE HILL, I'M SCARED AS HELL RIGHT NOW.

THOUGH WE SURE DO APPRECIATE HOW MANY JOBS WAYNE INDUSTRIES HAS CREATED IN THE TECHNOLOGY MARKET OVER THE YEARS...

...NOT TO MENTION YOUR *GOTHAM REVITALIZATION PLAN.*

WE AIM TO CREATE MORE, OF COURSE, *CONGRESSMAN.* I TRUST I'LL HAVE YOUR SUPPORT ON OUR AGREEMENT TO PURCHASE WITH THE CHINESE?

YOU JUST LET ME KNOW WHAT I CAN DO TO GREASE THE WHEELS, BRUCE. CALL MY OFFICE ON MONDAY, AND WE'LL CHAT A WHILE.

I'D LIKE TO SPEAK TO MR. WAYNE.

DO YOU HAVE AN APPOINTMENT, SIR?

I DON'T *NEED* AN APPOINTMENT.

I'M SORRY. HAVE WE MET, MR....?

*FORBES.*

INTERNAL AFFAIRS, GOTHAM P.D.

CITY OF GOTHAM POLICE DEPARTMENT INTERNAL AFFAIRS
LIEUTENANT
Forbes, J.

INTERNAL AFFAIRS? I'M SORRY, LIEUTENANT, YOU MAY HAVE ME CONFUSED WITH SOMEONE ELSE.

IF THIS IS ABOUT THAT PARKING TICKET OUTSIDE THE OPERA HOUSE, I'M CERTAIN MY ASSISTANT PAID IT--

I HEARD YOUR SPEECH TONIGHT, MR. WAYNE. WOULD'VE THOUGHT A MAN OF YOUR STATURE COULD AFFORD BETTER WRITERS.

THE WAY I SEE IT, ONE GUY'S FEARLESSNESS IS ANOTHER MAN'S *RECKLESSNESS*.

ESPECIALLY WHEN IT COMES TO THE ILLICIT FUNDING OF A VIGILANTE.

LADIES... WOULD YOU PLEASE GIVE LIEUTENANT FORBES AND ME A MOMENT?

LET ME TELL YOU WHAT I KNOW, MR. WAYNE. I KNOW EVEN SOMEONE WITH *YOUR* RESOURCES COULDN'T SOLVE THE LOGISTICS OF FINANCING BATMAN AND HIS CRONIES UNLESS YOU HAD *HELP*.

THAT HELP'S GOTTA COME FROM *INSIDE* GOTHAM P.D. SOMEONE HIGH UP... I WANT TO KNOW *WHO*--

THIS IS A CHARITABLE EVENT, BOYS. AND CHARITY USUALLY BEGINS AND ENDS WITH A *SMILE*.

SO YOU'RE TOM HUDSON'S DAUGHTER? I KNEW YOUR FATHER JUST BEFORE THEY MADE HIM A DIPLOMATIC ATTACHÉ TO MUMBAI.

YOU MUST HAVE BEEN VERY YOUNG.

FLATTERY WILL GET YOU EVERYWHERE, MISS HUDSON. AND I'VE HEARD YOUR MOTHER IS JUST AS BEAUTIFUL AS YOU.

OOH. FLATTERY WILL GET YOU *EVERYWHERE*, MR. WAYNE.

CALL ME *BRUCE*. YOU KNOW, YOUR DAD WAS ALWAYS FULL OF SURPRISES, BUT MARRYING A BOLLYWOOD ACTRESS...

...OVER HERE IN THE STATES, WE CALL IT "OUTPUNTING HIS COVERAGE." MEANT IN THE NICEST POSSIBLE WAY, OF COURSE.

I'M FAMILIAR WITH THE VERNACULAR. I'VE ATTENDED SCHOOL HERE SINCE I WAS NINE. BUT JUST SO YOU KNOW, MY MOTHER GOT THE BETTER END OF THAT DEAL.

TELL ME-- DO YOU THINK YOU COULD OUTPUNT *ME*, BRUCE?

I'M NOT SURE WHAT YOU MEAN, JAI.

I'LL LET YOU THINK ABOUT IT WHILE I CIRCULATE WITH THE GUESTS.

LET'S HOPE WE RUN INTO EACH OTHER AGAIN.

WELL, BRUCE...

...WHY DON'T YOU TRY TO *CATCH* ME?

TROUBLE, MASTER BRUCE?

NO DOUBT YOUR MIND IS *ALIVE* WITH THE POSSIBILITIES, *ALFRED.*

...NO, I SAID, "GET THIS TV CREW OUT OF MY FACE BEFORE I ACCIDENTALLY DISCHARGE MY WEAPON IN THEIR DIRECTION!"

WHAT THE HELL IS GOING *ON* AROUND HERE?!

SOMEONE TELL ME HOW COME THREE HUNDRED INMATES ON LOCKDOWN JUST BUGGED OUT AND BROKE FREE OF THEIR *UNBREAKABLE* RESTRAINTS?

CONTROL, I DON'T GIVE A RAT'S REAR END ABOUT PROTOCOL! I GOT SIXTY-FIVE GOOD MEN IN THERE, AN' WE ARE *NOT* WAITING FOR PERMISSION TO GO IN AFTER THEM--

*SARGE!* WE GOT HEAVY ACTIVITY BEHIND THE MAIN DOOR.

I GUESS OUR PERMISSION JUST ARRIVED.

I'LL CALL YOU BACK.

TWO-FACE. WHERE IS HE?

MAXIMUM SECURITY. H-HE DIDN'T COME OUT WITH THE OTHERS.

THEN WE GO IN AND *FIND* HIM. COME WITH ME.

YOU HEARD THE MAN.

FINCH
FRIEND
SINC'

A WHITE RABBIT?

IT'S A COMMON VISUAL MOTIF AMONG ABDUCTION VICTIMS, APPARENTLY. WHO WOULDA KNOWN?

HERE...WE FOUND THESE ALL ACROSS THE FACILITY. SOMEONE WASN'T EXACTLY SHY ABOUT HIDING THEM. SEND ME THE RESULTS WHEN YOU GET IT ANALYZED.

DID ANYONE MENTION SEEING A GIRL?

THIRTY-SEVEN INJURED. SEVEN IN CRITICAL CONDITION. FIFTEEN DEAD. AND YOU COULD'VE BEEN NUMBER SIXTEEN.

SHOULD'VE BEEN, JIM.

I GUESS TWO-FACE FINALLY DID SOMETHING RIGHT.

SPEAKING OF WHICH, A COUPLE OF THE OTHER INMATES ARE CLAIMING THEY WERE INJECTED WITH SOMETHING.

THE ONES STILL ALIVE AREN'T IN GOOD SHAPE. ONE OF THEM SAYS HE SAW A WHITE RABBIT FOR PETE'S SAKE.

PLEASE TELL ME YOU'RE NOT SERIOUS.

LOOK, ALL I KNOW IS WE'VE GOT A MESS ON OUR HANDS--THREE INMATES WHOSE BRAINS HAVE TURNED TO MUSH, AND WE'RE ABOUT TO GET HIT WITH MULTIPLE LAWSUITS FROM MULTIPLE DIRTBAG LAWYERS.

"THE ONLY ONE IN ANY SHAPE TO TALK IS TWO-FACE, BUT HE HASN'T SAID ANYTHING COHERENT SINCE HE CONVENIENTLY STARTED BLEEDING OUT OF HIS EYEBALLS."

EARLY ANALYSIS SUGGESTS THE CHEMICAL COMPOSITION IS RELATED TO THE FEAR TOXIN USED BY THE SCARECROW. THERE ARE ENOUGH SIMILARITIES TO SUGGEST THEY'RE RELATED.

THAT'S A START. HIS LAST KNOWN WHEREABOUTS?

HE WAS IN ARKHAM FOR A SHORT TIME, SIR.

"I'LL RUN THE FULL ANALYSIS AND HAVE THE RESULTS UPLOADED INTO THE BATMOBILE. IN THE MEANTIME, A FEW SMALL MATTERS REQUIRING YOUR ATTENTION...

"LUNCHEON WITH CONGRESSMAN STRICKER?"

"REGRETS. MY REGARDS TO HIS WIFE."

"TICKETS TO THE WORLD SERIES, GAME FIVE?"

"REGRETS. WITH GRATITUDE."

"DINNER WITH MISS JAINA HUDSON?"

"REGRETS...NO, ACCEPT. ANYTHING ELSE?"

"APART FROM THE IMPENDING APOCALYPSE, MASTER BRUCE, I DO BELIEVE WE'RE COVERED..."

"WE'VE FOUND THE INDIVIDUAL YOU'RE LOOKING FOR."

"PRECISELY SEVEN MINUTES AGO, NEWS CAME THROUGH THAT THE JOKER HAS COMMANDEERED A COMMUTER TRAIN HEADING NORTH OUT OF GOTHAM. THERE HAS BEEN NO WORD FROM ANYONE ON BOARD."

"THE JOKER'S BACK ALREADY? TELL GOTHAM PD I'M HEADED THAT WAY NOW."

"UNDERSTOOD. I'LL SEND WORD AHEAD THROUGH OUR USUAL CHANNELS."

"FURTHER ANALYSIS OF THE SAMPLE YOU PROVIDED CONFIRMS OUR INITIAL TEST RESULTS. SOMEONE SEEMS TO HAVE FASHIONED A DRUG CAPABLE OF LITERALLY REMOVING *FEAR* FROM A PERSON'S MIND."

"BUT IT COMES AT A PRICE--THE HUMAN BODY TRIES TO REJECT THE DRUG'S EFFECTS. HENCE THE SUDDEN FLOW OF BLOOD TO THE EYES AND NASAL MEMBRANES OF THOSE LESS FORTUNATE."

"OF COURSE, I SUPPOSE THEY'RE QUITE USED TO IT, CONSIDERING YOU EXTRACT THEIR BLOOD ON A *REGULAR BASIS...*"

**CATCH ME IF YOU CAN**
PAUL JENKINS writer/co-plotter  DAVID FINCH penciller/co-plotter  RICHARD FRIEND inker
cover art by DAVID FINCH, RICHARD FRIEND & ALEX SINCLAIR

HRAHH!

EXIT

HHH... DON'T GET USED TO THAT RUSH OF BLOOD TO THE HEAD. WHEN IT WEARS OFF, IT'S GOING TO COME OUT OF YOUR *EYES*--

ON THE CONTRARY, MY DEAR ONION, I FEEL FINE. AND QUITE STABLE, CONSIDERING I'M AS HABITUALLY UNSTABLE AS A RABID HONEY BADGER SURFING ON A JELLY VOLCANO.

MY LOVELY YOUNG LADY FRIEND HERE TELLS ME THE TWERPS IN THE NUTHOUSE WERE JUST A *TEST*.

I GET THE NEW AND IMPROVED FORMULA. SAYS SO ON THE LABEL.

TOO BAD IT DOESN'T WORK ON YOUR *ACTING* SKILLS.

THE *REAL* JOKER IS PREDOMINANTLY LEFT-HANDED, BY THE WAY.

YOU'RE MISTAKEN, BATS, I'M...

...I'M NOT...

...NNOOOTTTT FFUUNNYY!

IT'S ALWAYS THE SAME STORY WITH YOU, CLAYFACE...*EHH*...YOU TRY SO HARD TO BE OTHER PEOPLE...

*~HFSS~* BUT YOU NEVER CAN KEEP IT *TOGETHER*...

CLANG

I *LIKE* YOU.

WHY, MR. WAYNE! WHAT KIND OF GIRL DO YOU TAKE ME FOR?

AND HERE I WAS THINKING YOU WERE A RESPECTABLE CITIZEN! FOR SHAME!

NOTHING UNTOWARD, JAI, I PROMISE--

--I'M SORRY. WOULD YOU EXCUSE ME FOR A MOMENT, PLEASE?

BZZZ BZZZ

White Rabbit spotted four minutes ago near Robbinsville. Trust this puts question to rest. -A

IS EVERYTHING OKAY? I HOPE IT WASN'T BAD NEWS.

ON THE CONTRARY-- EVERYTHING'S FINE. CRISIS AVERTED.

WELL, THANK GOD FOR SMALL MERCIES AND LACE PANTIES.

NOW...ARE YOU INTERESTED IN DESSERT?

VANDALS AND VISIGOTHS AT THE GATES. LUNATICS ON EVERY CORNER AND NARY ENOUGH TIME TO CAPTURE ONE BEFORE *ANOTHER* APPEARS.

BUT ONE MUST START SOMEWHERE. A CUP OF *TEA*, PERHAPS?

I'VE NEVER SEEN ANYTHING REMOTELY THIS COMPLEX. ITS COMPOSITE STRUCTURE IS BASED ON SCARECROW'S FEAR TOXIN BUT IT ACTS *DIFFERENTLY*.

THIS SUBSTANCE EFFECTIVELY DESENSITIZES THE AMYGDALA AND HYPOTHALAMUS, REMOVING A SUBJECT'S FIGHT-OR-FLIGHT MECHANISM FROM THE EQUATION. INSTEAD OF SENDING YOU INTO A PARALYSIS OF FEAR, IT SOMEHOW MAKES YOU *FEARLESS*.

HMFF. I'LL STICK TO MY TEA.

NINETY-NINE PERCENT PROBABILITY IT COMES FROM THIS--THE VIRGIN STAR CACTUS, DISTANTLY RELATED TO PEYOTE AND ALSO ONE OF THE RAREST PLANTS ON EARTH.

THE SUBJECT BECOMES FLOODED WITH ADRENALINE, AND EVENTUALLY THE BODY BREAKS DOWN... VENOUS AND LYMPHATIC SYSTEMS... EVEN ARTERIES. HENCE THE BLEEDING EYEBALLS.

INDEED. DID WE MANAGE TO ISOLATE THE SECONDARY COMPOUND IN THIS MARVELOUS POISON?

POISON *IVY*.

SNACKS AT THIS HOUR?

PEOPLE DRINK GINSENG TEA TO HONE THEIR POWERS OF CONCENTRATION, SIR. I, ON THE OTHER HAND, HAVE *ICE CREAM*.

IT'S SOME KIND OF ACCESS CODE TO A BIO-ELECTRONIC RELAY SYSTEM--

*ICE* CREAM, SIR.

IVY'S CODE IS BASED ON AN ANCIENT CIPHER ATTRIBUTED TO FOLLOWERS OF DEMETER.

THE GREEK GODDESS OF *PLANTS*, IF I REMEMBER MY CLASSICAL LITERATURE.

GPS PUTS HER ON HARMON ISLAND, ABOUT SEVEN MILES OFF THE COAST. IT'S BASICALLY SWAMPLAND OWNED BY THE GOVERNMENT. NO ONE'S LIVED THERE FOR FIFTY YEARS.

INITIATE THE SAFETY RECHECKS ON THE *BAT-PLANE*.

IVY KNOWS MY SYSTEMS CAN TABULATE TO PINPOINT HER CHLORO-PHEROMONE SIGNAL.

She's right. Let them hold the fort while you get to the source.

The only way to **stop** this is to find the person **behind** it.

Not the White Rabbit. She's a pawn or a wild card, but she's not the type.

Your perp is a control freak. A fearmonger.

But he underestimates others. He needed Ivy to perfect his toxin, but he doesn't **know** her--and that's his first mistake.

She's smarter than most. Not the kind to be taken lightly or **easily**.

"TEN TIPS FOR A HAPPY **DOG**," IVY?

GOOD **GIRL**.

HANDFUL OF DUST
PAUL JENKINS writer/co-plotter   DAVID FINCH penciller/co-plotter   RICHARD FRIEND inker
cover art by DAVID FINCH, RICHARD FRIEND & ALEX SINCLAIR

BLACK WITH TWO SUGARS, JUST LIKE YOU--

NOT NOW.

WHAT WAS THAT, COMMISSIONER?

NOT YOU, FORBES.

I HAVE TO TALK TO YOU WHENEVER YOU SAY, ISN'T THAT RIGHT?

YOU'RE ENTITLED TO COUNSEL. I THINK IT'S PROBABLY IN YOUR BEST INTEREST TO SPEAK WITH A LAWYER BEFORE A HEARING IS SCHED--

LAWYER?

I RUN THE DAMN POLICE DEPARTMENT, YOU LITTLE STAIN. AND WE'RE IN THE MIDDLE OF ONE OF THE WORST INMATE UPRISINGS THIS CITY HAS EVER SEEN!

NOW YOU LISTEN TO ME, LIEUTENANT...I RUN AS TIGHT A SHIP AS I CAN AND YOU HAVE NO IDEA HOW CHOPPY THE WATERS GET OUT HERE.

SO UNLESS YOU'RE READY TO SPROUT A PAIR AND TAKE ON SOME ACTUAL BAD GUYS FOR ONCE, YOU'LL LEAVE ME TO MY ULCER, MY NICOTINE ADDICTION AND MY COMMITMENT TO MAKING SURE THE CITIZENS OF GOTHAM CITY AND MY MEN DON'T SUFFER FOR SOME FOOL CRUSADE YOU'VE--

WHY DON'T YOU ASK BATMAN FOR HELP?

I TOLD YOU, I DON'T KNOW WHAT YOU'RE--

LAWYER UP, COMMISSIONER. YOU EARNED THAT RIGHT.

SONOFA--

WHAT IS IT, DETECTIVE?

WE'VE HERDED THE LAST OF THE ARKHAM INMATES BACK INTO CUSTODY.

OKAY. WHAT ELSE?

BRANSTON

YOU ASKED ABOUT BATMAN...IF ANY-ONE HAD SEEN HIM LATELY.

AND...?

THAT'S A NEGATIVE, SIR...

"...WE DON'T KNOW *WHERE* HE IS."

I'M *ALMOST* DISAPPOINTED, BATMAN.

YOU'RE MEANT TO BE THIS GREAT *INVESTIGATOR*--THE *WORLD'S GREATEST DETECTIVE*, SO THEY SAY.

AND YOU CAN'T EVEN *DEDUCE* YOUR WAY OUT OF A *CHILDREN'S BOOK!*

The *White Rabbit* is a guide into a story about *nonsense*.

Each character to follow in *Alice's Adventures in Wonderland* is more outlandish and makes less sense than the last.

Most think the Rabbit is as *loony* as the others, checking his *watch* and afraid of how *late* he is.

HEE!

But he's actually *terrified* of losing his *head*.

I'VE CIRCLED THE PLANET... **SIX TIMES** SINCE BATMAN SENT ME RUNNING.

WHAT ELSE... CAN I **DO?**

THINK OF IT LIKE A **SNAKE BITE.**

WE NEED TO **FIND** A WAY TO GET THE **VENOM** OUT OF YOUR BLOODSTREAM.

**WAIT A SECOND--** DID YOU SAY **VENOM?**

BATMAN'S GOT IT ALL **WRONG...**

"...WE NEED TO GET **BACK!**"

WHAT WAS SCARECROW **AFTER** HERE?

TWO-FACE... POISON IVY...CLAYFACE... I'VE TAKEN THEM DOWN A **DOZEN TIMES.** I FEAR WHAT ALL OF THEM ARE **CAPABLE** OF.

BUT I'M **NOT** GOING SOFT ON ANY OF THEM **NOW.**

NO...WE WOULDN'T **EXPECT** THAT.

HA!

IT'S JUST A MATTER OF *TIME*, BATMAN.

"YOU'VE GOT TO
KEEP *GOING!*"

**WAMM**

BANE'S TOXIN COULDN'T GAIN A FOOTHOLD AGAINST YOUR METABOLISM.

YOU PUSHED THROUGH THE BARRIER, JUST LIKE BATMAN PREDICTED.

EHH...

...LOOK...I'M GONNA BE FINE. I NEED TO GET BACK TO BATMAN.

I CAN'T ALLOW THAT, FLASH. WE HAVE TO GET YOU TO A *HOSPITAL*--

I MAY HAVE BEEN RUNNING AROUND IN CIRCLES FOR A COUPLE OF DAYS...

...BUT I DIDN'T LOSE MY SENSE OF *DIRECTION*.

Failure.

NO...
IT'S NOT
POSSIBLE!

I'M
STRONGER
THAN YOU!

NO...

PAK

...YOU'RE
NOT.

There's something about *Gotham City* that brings it out in you.

The worst we're all capable of.

"COMMUTERS DISCOVERED THE SCENE AND CALLED IT IN. GOTTA FIGURE *MOST* MORNINGS THEY'RE PISSED THE TRAIN IS RUNNING *LATE*.

POLICE LINE DO NOT CROSS

"IMAGINE WHAT THEY THOUGHT WHEN THEY SAW IT *WAITING* FOR THEM TODAY..."

OFTEN ENOUGH, WE GET TO PUSH THIS ALL OFF ON THE *FREAKS* AND THE *MANIACS* AND THE SO-CALLED MASTER-MINDS OF CRIME.

BUT I'LL LET YOU SEE FOR *YOUR-SELF*.

THEN YOU TELL *ME* WHAT WE'RE DEALING WITH DOWN HERE.

We work in *extremes* here in Gotham.

Sociopaths, terrorists, rogues, and super-villains.

Sometimes it numbs us to the smaller horrors.

But it's important to remember...

...what a good look in the *mirror* can reveal.

THE MADNESS

BLUNT FORCE TRAUMA TO THE SKULL.

MULTIPLE FRACTURES AND STAB WOUNDS. AND THE *OBVIOUS* LOSS OF BLOOD.

SAME AS THE OTHERS AROUND THE CITY, GORDON.

I HAD A FEELING THE SECOND I SAW THE SCENE.

THIS WASN'T SOME DIABOLICAL *SPREE* LAUNCHED BY DE-RANGED MEMBERS OF YOUR *ROGUES GALLERY.*

THEY DID THIS TO *THEMSELVES.*

THE *WEST HARLOW STATION* WAS BUILT ALMOST ONE HUNDRED YEARS AGO.

OLD CITY PLANNING MAPS INDICATE MYRIAD PASSAGES AND TRACK LENGTHS THAT HAVE BEEN CLOSED FOR ALMOST THAT LONG.

YOU ARE SUGGESTING GOTHAM'S CITIZENS *ARE NOT* ATTEMPTING TO KILL ONE ANOTHER.

AND YOU *ASSUME* THE ANSWER IS UNDERGROUND.

I NEED TO BELIEVE WE HAVEN'T REACHED THAT PRECIPICE YET, ALFRED.

AND IF THERE *IS* SOMETHING HAPPENING IN THOSE TUNNELS MAKING PEOPLE ATTACK EACH OTHER--

--I NEED TO *DISCOVER* IT BEFORE IT HAPPENS AGAIN.

YOU KNOW, COMMISSIONER, THERE'S A *TERM* WE USE DOWN AT *INTERNAL AFFAIRS* FOR COPS WHO GO OFF THE RESERVATION AND OPERATE BY THEIR OWN RULES.

*CRIMINALS.*

GIVE IT A REST, *LIEUTENANT FORBES.* THERE AREN'T ANY CAMERAS OR POLITICIANS AROUND.

AND *I'M* NOT IN THE DAMN MOOD.

MAYBE IF YOU PUT IN SOME *STREET TIME* YOU'D UNDERSTAND.

OR MAYBE I NEED TO BRING SOME OF THESE *POLITICIANS* INTO THIS.

AS IT HAPPENS, THE RIGHT AND HONORABLE MAYOR OF GOTHAM CITY HAS SEEN FIT TO APPROVE MY REQUEST TO HAVE YOUR MENTAL AND EMOTIONAL *STABILITY* EVALUATED.

YOU'RE SENDING *ME* TO A SHRINK?

IF YOU THINK I'M GOING TO--

I KNOW I FEEL *BETTER* ALREADY.

YOU'LL *GO,* COMMISSIONER. YOU'LL UNBURDEN YOURSELF OF RECENT PROBLEMS AND REGRETS.

AND THEN WE'LL *REVISIT* YOUR CASE FILE.

SNAP

POLICE LINE DO NOT CROSS

THERE SHOULD BE AN UNFINISHED CORRIDOR UP AHEAD, MASTER BRUCE.

GOTHAM TRANSIT *CLOSED* IT DECADES AGO AFTER SOME RENOVATIONS TO THE LINE.

I SEE IT, ALFRED.

AND IT LOOKS LIKE I'M NOT THE *ONLY* ONE WHO HAS.

I'M MOVING INTO THE ADJACENT TUNNEL. IF WE LOSE OUR *SIGNAL*, LET'S HOPE THAT'S THE REASON--

RRRRMMMMBBBBLL

MASTER BRUCE? ARE YOU STILL THERE?

I'M HERE.

A PASSING *TRAIN* JUST SHOOK THE TUNNEL.

BUT I'M NOT SHOWING *ANY* TRAINS IN YOUR VICINITY, SIR...

LOOK, DUMPSON... A LITTLE BAT.

>HNNF<

The cousins *Dumpson* and *Deever Tweed* have made mischief in this city for a few years now...

CATCH.

...but I've never seen them like this.

THOK

YOU PLAYED IT WRONGLY, COUSIN. INSTEAD OF *TOYING* WITH VERMIN--

RRRG...

WHUDD

--IT'S BEST TO JUST *SQUISH* THEM!

They hit like *trucks* and make just as much noise.

MASTER BRUCE--?! ARE YOU ALL RIGHT?

I JUST GOT TRAMPLED →HNNG← BY OVERSIZED *BEDTIME STORIES*, ALFRED...

ONLY MY *EGO* IS BRUISED.

IF THE TWEED COUSINS WERE UNDER THE SAME *CONTROL* AS THE SUBWAY PASSENGERS, WHAT MIGHT IT MEAN...

...FOR THE *REST* OF GOTHAM?

--A BUZZ IN THE AIR HERE IN SOUTH CITY PARK AS *SENATOR TOOMEY* IS EXPECTED TO ANNOUNCE HIS INTENTION TO SEEK THE *PRESIDENCY* TODAY.

HE'S MAKING HIS WAY TO THE *PODIUM* NOW.

LET'S LISTEN TO THE SENATOR...

GOTHAM CITY IS A SYMBOL OF AMERICAN RESILIENCE AND ASPIRATION, AND I AM CONTINUALLY *INSPIRED* BY ITS MAJESTY, ALONG WITH ITS TOUGHNESS.

WHICH IS WHY I STAND BEFORE YOU TODAY TO ANNOUNCE MY CANDIDACY...

...FOR *PRESIDENT*...

OH MY GOD! IT APPEARS THE SENATOR JUST PULLED A *GUN* AT THE PODIUM!

...OF THE UNITED--

BLAM

POLICE EMERGENCY CHANNELS ARE SWAMPED WITH CALLS CONCERNING IRRATIONAL PEOPLE DOING *FRIGHTENING* THINGS.

HOW CAN YOU BE CERTAIN THE *TWEEDS* DIDN'T KILL ANYONE?

DEE AND DUM MIGHT HAVE BEEN AFFECTED BY WHATEVER'S DRIVING PEOPLE OFF THE DEEP END, BUT THOSE SUBWAY VICTIMS KILLED *THEMSELVES.*

THE FORENSICS WILL PROVE THAT.

BUT SURELY THE TWEEDS WEREN'T INNOCENT BYSTANDERS?

MOST *DEFINITELY* NOT.

BUT BEFORE THEY BLEW UP THE TUNNEL AND ESCAPED, I DETECTED A FAINT BROADCAST ON AN UNUSUAL FREQUENCY.

YES...SPECTRUM ANALYSIS MATCHES A TRANSMISSION ORIGINATING FROM THE COORDINATES I AM SENDING OVER NOW.

SEND THEM TO GORDON. HAVE HIM MEET ME THERE.

ALL TOO OFTEN IT WOULD SEEM, MASTER BRUCE...

WHERE THE *HENCHMEN* SCURRY HOME TO, THE *BOSS* IS OFTEN WAITING.

Jervis Tetch has a fancy for mind control and manipulation.

As the Mad Hatter, he's devoted himself to spreading his bizarre strain of chaos every time he hits the open air.

I AM THE TALON OF THE COURT OF OWLS.

I AM THEIR WEAPON.

HE IS LINCOLN MARCH, A MAYORAL CANDIDATE FOR GOTHAM CITY.

HE IS MY TARGET.

BUT THIS MAN IS NOT WITHOUT RESOURCES.

I CANNOT ONLY FAULT MY CARELESSNESS.

MY BODY IS FAILING ME MUCH IN THE WAY IT WAS DETERIORATING BEFORE I WAS PUT INTO THE COLD SLEEP.

I AM OLD.

AND I AM SLOW TO REACT. UNPREPARED FOR THE UNEXPECTED.

LIKE THIS SHADOW THAT FALLS BEFORE ME.

I THINK, "WHO IS THIS?"

**HELP!**

**PLEASE, HELLLLP!**

I SHOUTED FOR WHAT FELT LIKE A DAY.

THEN...THE HEAT OF THE FLAMES FADED.

I FELT COLD.

SOMETHING DIED.

AND SOMETHING WAS **BORN**.

ALL THE RINGMASTER SAID WAS, "YOU ARE WORTHY TO BE THE NEXT **TALON**."

BUT I WAS A **TALON**. AND I LIVED **WITHOUT FEAR**.

AND I WAS TO PERFORM **WITHOUT FAILURE**.

HOWEVER, MY EXCURSION TO THE CIRCUS COST ME TIME AND FORCED ME TO CHANGE PLANS.

MY ATTACK WAS OUT ON THE STREETS.

IT WAS THERE THAT I MET SOMETHING **NEW** TO GOTHAM.

AND FOR THE SECOND TIME THAT NIGHT...

...I FELT AFRAID.

THEN, YEARS LATER...

...THE SLEEP ENDED.

AND NOT JUST FOR ME...

...BUT FOR **ALL** OF THE TALONS. ALL WHO BORE THE MANTLE.

THE COURT IS NOW STRIKING **GOTHAM** WITH ITS MIGHTY CLAWS IN **ONE NIGHT.** ALL OF ITS ENEMIES. ALL OF ITS IMPEDIMENTS.

ALL WHO STAND IN THE WAY OF THE COURT OF OWLS--SHALL FALL.

HE IS **LINCOLN MARCH.**

A **MAYORAL** CANDIDATE FOR GOTHAM CITY.

GOD ALMIGHTY--

HE IS MY **TARGET.**

I HAVE NO IDEA **WHY HE**
IS TO BE KILLED. IT IS NEVER
A TALON'S PLACE TO ASK.
HE IS JUST ANOTHER **DROP**
ADDED TO THE **GALLONS** OF
BLOOD I HAVE SPILLED.

IT IS **OVER**. ALL THAT YOU
WERE. ALL THAT YOU
WILL BE. IT IS **DONE**.

D-DAMN
YOU--

BUT MY YEARS--MY
LONG NIGHTS--HAVE
DULLED MY BLADES.

I AM
**WEAK**.

AND MY PAST
FAILURES FALL
UPON ME LIKE
SHADOWS.

IT IS OVER.

NOTHINGNESS COMES.

AND FOR THE SMALLEST ETERNITY...

...THERE IS PEACE.

BUT I RETURN...

...AND SEE WHAT HAS HAUNTED ME. WHAT HAS DRIVEN ME HERE.

IT IS NOT A THING.

IT IS A MAN.

I CAN KILL A MAN.